AF499349

BUILD YOUR OWN COMPUTER FROM SCRATCH

Do it yourself guide in building or upgrading an existing computer plus installation of operating system,

(The tested & trusted guide for beginner's)

BY,

Engr. Wiley Louis

TABLE OF CONTENT

STAGE ONE

INTRODUCTION TO BUILDING A COMPUTER

Computer is an electronic machine that accepts data and give out information. The rate in which computer usage is high in our society today makes it a good plan for person to know how to build a computer for personal and business purposes.

Figuring out how to assemble a PC is overwhelming, yet sorting all the parts out is simpler than it might look. Generally, building a PC reduces to realizing where to connect your segments and links. In this guide, we will walk you through the way toward building a PC bit by bit, paying little mind to your experience or experience.

In the event that you are now acquainted with the general cycle of building a PC, you can leap to a particular advance utilizing the rundown beneath:

Introducing the force supply, introducing the processor, introducing the RAM, Installing the motherboard, introducing the CPU cooler, Install the illustrations card, introducing any development cards, Installing your capacity drives, Power on.

BEGINNING

This guide is tied in with sorting parts out to make a useful machine. In the event that you haven't chose and bought all the necessary equipment, ensure you do that first. It's additionally a smart thought to buy your case last so you can ensure all that will fit inside it.

THE PARTS IS READY THEN FOLLOW UP THE PC ASSEMBLY PROCESS

Before you dive in, guarantee there's a tidy up workspace with a lot of space to open boxes and set up parts. Ideally, there's now a heap before you. If not, our PC assemble guide can walk you through that cycle.

There are a few wellbeing issues to examine before we really begin tearing open those crates.

HOW TO TORCH A PC TO AVOID SHOCK

There's an imperceptible danger when fabricating a PC that can pound the most remarkable framework: Static power. The very power that allows you to stun your companions when you wear fleece socks can likewise sear segments instantly. Luckily, static is not difficult to everything except wipe out with a couple of basic advances.

One straightforward arrangement is to buy an enemy of static wristband. One end folds over your wrist, and different clasps some place on the PC case, keeping the wearer continually grounded. Contacting the case often with the PSU connected and controlled off accomplishes a similar impact.

Aside from that,

- form your PC in a stay with an exposed floor
- rugs create a ton of static
- Wear elastic soled shoes instead of socks.

A large number boat in enemy of static packs, so leave them sacked until not long before establishment.

This guide fills in as an overall outline of the cycle, and the guidelines pressed with your parts may differ from our proposals. This is a general manual for the undertaking.

OPENING THE CASE

Setting up the case is the simple part. Directions for the particular case you bought ought to acquaint you with its essential design just as rundown unique guidelines with respect to segment establishment.

Set out the case in your work zone and eliminate the side board. For most PC cases, this implies the left-side board when seen from the front. This board gives admittance to the case inside.

Additionally, eliminate whatever's hanging inside the situation. On the off chance that it's joined, push it aside. Numerous cases have perpetual interior wiring that gets hazardous later on.

Before we begin assembling everything, we'll initially introduce the force supply and afterward put the case in a safe spot for a couple of moments.

REQUIRED TOOLS NEEDED TO BUILD A COMPUTER

Building your own computer from scratch requires some useful tool to execute such task. These tools are easily available in a nearby electronics store. The tools listed below are what you need to build your personal computer;

A. SCREW DRIVER

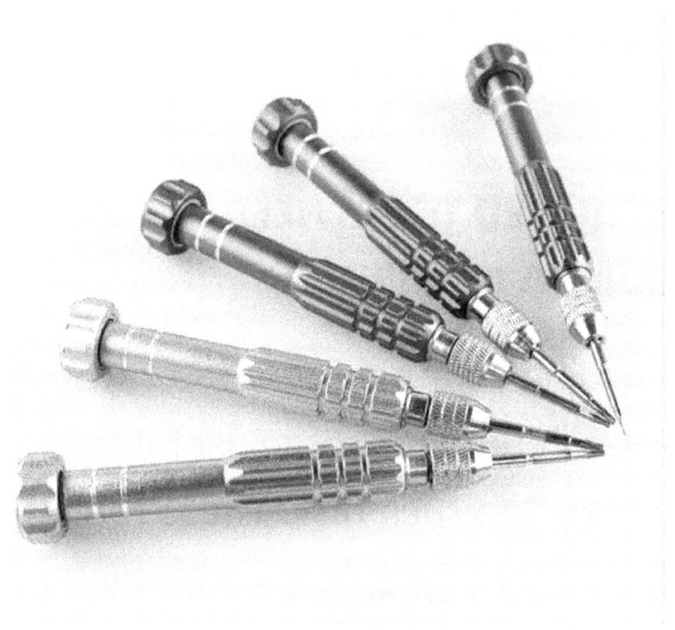

This is the major tools needed in building a computer. The screw on the computer casing can be tightening with a screw driver for it to be well secure. The screw driver should be the shorter and longer type since it serves different purposes. A Philips head size screw driver is preferred for this job. Avoid magnetic screw driver because if not properly handled, it might affect the electronics component during installations.

B. ANTI-STATIC WRIST STRAP

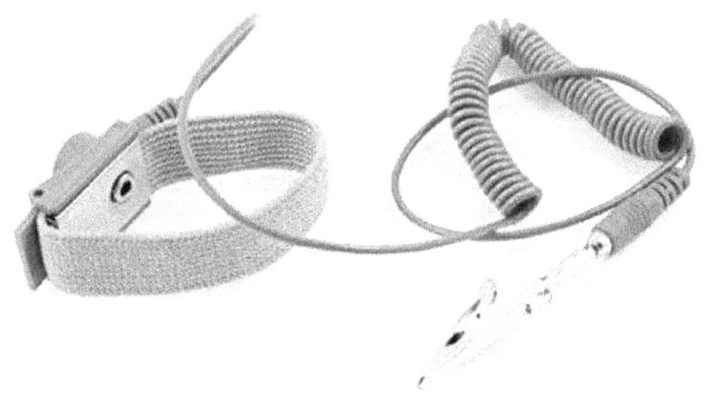

This is a bracelet device that is place on the wrist. It anti-static property helps for the reduction of electric discharge from human body to the computer component. it is connected to electric current so as to neutralize any electric current generating on the human body.

C. CABLE TIES

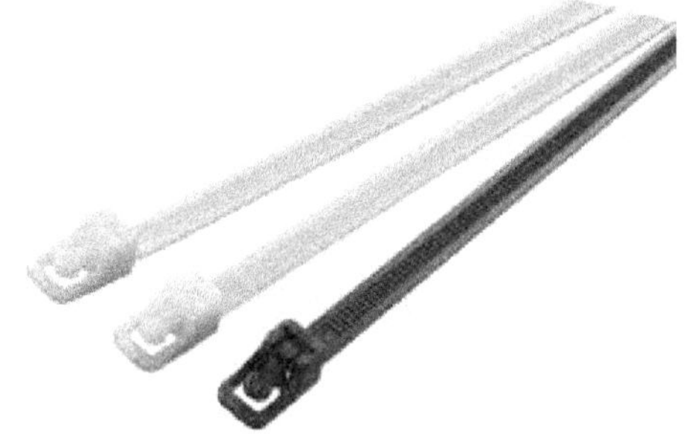

It is used to tie together any loose cable within the computer casing so as to give your finished work a good look. Computer cases are mainly shipped together with cable ties so buying one might not be needed.

D. FLASH LIGHT

Flash light is need if your working environment is getting dark than you can see clearly. It is difficult to work on some computer casing within getting an external flash light due to their interior make.

E. NEEDLE NOSE PLIER

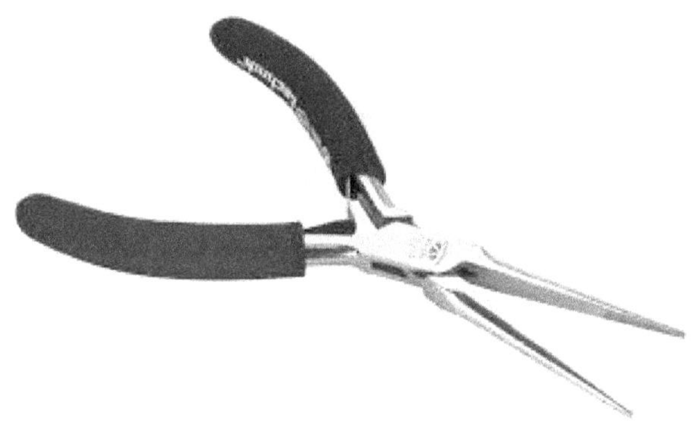

Bolt or not that proves hard to lose are taking care of with the use of pier. You can also use the pliers to pick screws that are hidden in a place that your hand can not reach.

F. POWER METER

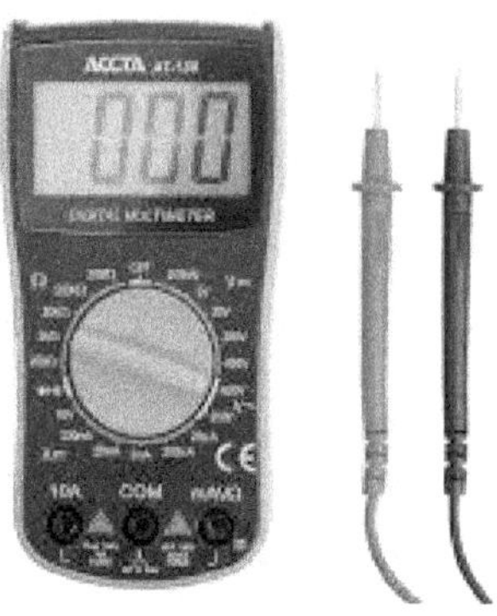

This meter is use to test for continuity of the conductor you are using. The voltage and current your computer will be using can also be check with this device.

STAGE TWO

Install the force supply

The initial part to advance into the case ought to be the force supply (PSU). It is normally situated at the back of the case, as a rule in the base or top corner.

If all else fails, the space is handily situated via looking for a square opening with screw openings in any event two corners. The PSU sits in this opening with its force switch and a female attachment looking out from the case's back board. Counsel your case's manual on the off chance that you experience difficulty finding the legitimate area.

You can introduce the force supply with the fan looking up or down. In most PC cases, pointing the fan down is ideal. You should simply take a gander at your case. In the event that there's space between the base and floor (and ideally a residue channel in the middle), introduce your force supply with the fan looking down. Most current cases are worked for this kind of establishment. On the off chance that your case manual says something other than what's expected, in any case, we suggest following that.

There are two fundamental force supply variations: Standard and particular. There's a cross breed semi-particular sort as well, yet we don't have to stress over that for the time being.

Secluded PSUs have links that separate from the principle unit to dodge mess. They're ideal for more modest cases and flawless oddities. On the off chance that you have a measured PSU, it's ideal to forget about the links until further notice and run them as you introduce each extra segment.

On the off chance that the PSU's links don't confine, cautiously pack them so they're hanging out the case's open side board. This incidentally keeps them far removed while we introduce the excess parts.

STAGE THREE

Install the processor

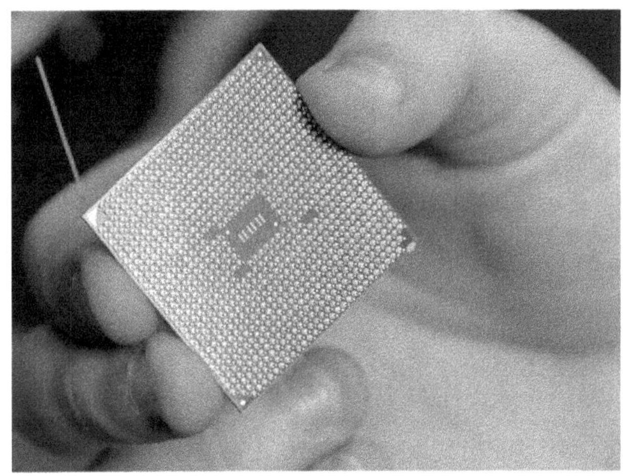

Then, set up the motherboard by introducing the CPU and RAM prior to fitting it for the situation. They're much simpler to introduce now as opposed to after the motherboard dwells in the framework

Indeed, contingent upon your case and cooler, you will be unable to gather your framework with the motherboard as of now introduced. That is on the grounds that numerous reseller's exchange coolers utilize a backplate to give the most impenetrable fit conceivable. It is, obviously, joined to the rear of the motherboard. You won't have the option to introduce it except if you have a case with a cut-out that lines up with the backplate's area, an element commonly discovered uniquely in top of the line nooks.

There are various pins on the CPU and motherboard, and bowing any of them could deliver that segment dead.

Cautiously eliminate the motherboard from its enemy of static pack and set it on a hard, level, non-metal surface, for example, a wooden work area, or the highest point of the motherboard box itself. Additionally, ensure there are no wellsprings of residue or fluid close by.

Despite the fact that introducing a CPU is a simpler errand now than it was in earlier years, it's as yet perhaps the most unstable. There are various pins on the CPU and motherboard, and bowing any of them could deliver that segment dead.

All things considered, the cycle isn't intended to be troublesome, and as long as you adhere to the guidelines plainly and look out to guarantee the chip is completely situated before you clasp it set up, you'll be fine. In any case, there are some unpretentious contrasts in the process contingent upon who made your CP.

Rather than extending from the processor, sticks presently dwell in current Intel attachments on motherboards, making CPU establishment simple. This piece of the attachment is known as the contact cluster. Totally don't curve or contact these pins!

The square metal section holding the CPU set up is the heap plate, and it's raised and brought down utilizing the heap switch. At the point when cinched down, the finish of the heap switch tucks under a snare to keep everything set up. At the point when you unpack your motherboard, the contact exhibit will be covered with a piece of plastic. This plastic will jump out once you open the section, so hold back to open it until you're prepared to introduce your processor.

To start with, open the heap plate. Do this by tenderly pushing down on the heap arm and moving it out sideways from under the snare, and afterward raising it up as far as possible. The snare's switch activity opens the plate, which you can undoubtedly flip up. Now, the plastic piece will come free. In the event that it doesn't jump out, delicately eliminate it.

As demonstrated over, the actual CPU ought to have a little half-hover score on each side of the chip. With the contacts looking down, there ought to be just a single course where the scores line up with the indents in the attachment. Get your processor by the sides, clipping it daintily between your fingertips. Here, you need to try not to contact the lower part of the processor.

With the processor close by, line up the scores (or utilize the little gold triangle in the corner to arrange the attachment) and set the processor in.

You don't have to apply any power here. The processor should opening in without issues. When it's sitting in the attachment, tenderly press the side to ensure it opened in. Once more, delicately do this. You would prefer not to move your processor.

Utilize the heap arm as an afterthought to bring down the plate over the chip, at that point push down and re-cut the arm under the snare by and by. This requires a considerable lot of pressing factor, so ensure the chip is appropriately situated prior to pushing down.

Keep in mind, the indents in the processor ought to line up with those in the attachment. If all else fails, start again and twofold check.

Instructions to introduce an AMD processor

Dissimilar to Intel's plan, pins extend from AMD's CPUs. These pins embed into openings inserted in the motherboard's CPU attachment. The heap arm on the attachment marginally moves the openings under, holding the pins on the processor when squeezed right down.

On the off chance that it isn't as of now, raise the arm so that it's pointing straight up, and afterward rests somewhat farther back. That guarantees the openings for the pins are totally open.

Rather than utilizing indents, effectively line up the processor in the opening utilizing a triangle engraved in gold on one of the CPU's corners. You should simply arrange that triangle according to a subsequent triangle cut into the opening. Once more, gets the processor by the sides tenderly, staying away from the base.

When the processor sits easily in the space, essentially presses the arm down until it fits properly and secures. This last advance can be scary since it requires a considerable lot of strain to secure.

STAGE FOUR

Install the RAM

Framework memory, or RAM, doesn't need any cautious go situation or wires. There are only two significant elements, expecting you've picked viable RAM: Direction and opening decision.

The course is sufficiently simple. Every memory stick has a score in the contacts arranging the base edge that line with a square in the motherboard's memory spaces. In the event that you hold it simply over the opening and the two line up, it's confronting the correct course. In the event that it doesn't arrange, turn it 180 degrees.

Opening decision relies upon a couple of components, one of which is the way you bought RAM. In the event that it's simply a solitary stick, introduce it in the A1 opening and proceed onward with your life. A graph in the motherboard's manual should name the openings on the off chance that it isn't printed straightforwardly on the PCB.

Be that as it may, you probably bought two indistinguishable RAM sticks, a typical bundle called a double channel arrangement. The framework can utilize the two sticks as though they were a solitary square of RAM however gets to them exclusively, giving an unobtrusive lift to memory execution.

You ought to introduce these sticks in channels (openings) with coordinating tones, typically marked A1 and B1, however once in a while A2 and B2 are ideal. Check your motherboard's manual to affirm which are best for your framework.

Since we know the appropriate opening and heading, the following part is simple. Push the plastic wings at one or the flip side of the opening down and outward (some motherboards just have one) at that point place the stick in the space staying straight up. Push down immovably until the RAM clicks into the opening, and the plastic wings.

STAGE FIVE

Install the motherboard

Introducing your pressed motherboard is adequately simple; however it can't simply sit for your situation. Most current cases have implicit, non-removable spacers between the back divider and motherboard, known as stalemates. They go about as a ground for the motherboard while forestalling the associations on the back from shorting.

A few cases have removable deadlocks you should physically introduce. They're not difficult to recognize on the grounds that they look uncommon - basically screws that have another screw opening on top rather than the ordinary screwdriver indent. They're generally copper or gold in shading, making them simple to select

Your motherboard's direction relies upon your case. This is for the motherboard's I/O board — the part containing the USB, video, and Ethernet associations. Your motherboard ships with an I/O shield that finds a way into this rectangular cut-out. On the off chance that you introduce that shield and, at that point adjust your motherboard's I/O board, you should see the motherboard's screw openings line up with the deadlocks for your situation.

If not, you may have to squirm the motherboard somewhat to ensure it snaps appropriately into the I/O shield and the stands-offs adjust. This may require some exertion, yet it shouldn't need a lot of power. In case you're constraining the motherboard, twofold check how it's adjusted, as it may not be appropriately situated. Be firm yet delicate.

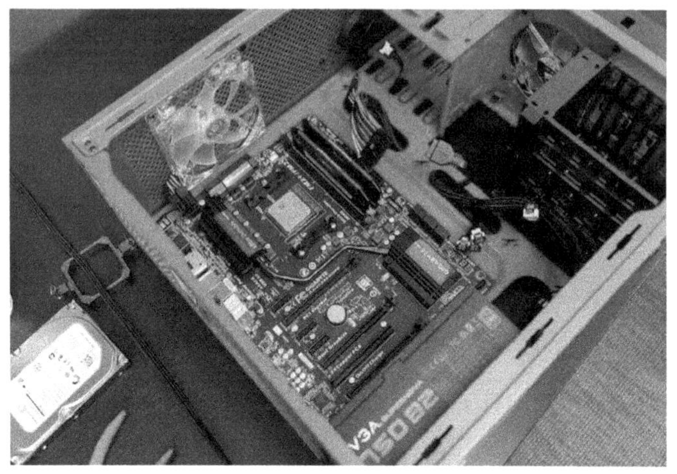

Try not to go wild while fixing screws, as you may harm the board on the off chance that you put in an excessive amount of exertion.

You may locate that not all openings coordinate with stalemates under. Drop a screw into an opening to check whether it strings immediately.

Like each set of screws, the initial step is seating the screws and giving them several preliminary turns. At that point, continue in a star design, fixing each screw a little at a time. Try not to go wild while fixing as you would harm the board. You just need enough force to hold the board set up without squirming.

When the motherboard situates serenely for the situation, there are a couple of fundamental associations.

To begin with, the motherboard's force association is a wide, two-column link that fits cozily into a comparable looking spot on the actual board. The motherboard plus the CPU can only get power from terminal 20 to 28. Nonetheless, a few sheets have a subsequent 4-pin or 8-pin connector for the processor, which dwells close to your CPU, normally in the top corner. In the event that you have it, you'll need to connect that, as well.

Second, associate the case attachments and catches to the motherboard. A twofold wide line of pins — the area of which will be noted in your manual — runs the USB ports, catches for reset and force, and movement LEDs for force and capacity.

These little links run in a group from any place the ports dwell for the situation. Legitimate establishment can be troublesome, nonetheless, because of their size. On the off chance that you have an amplifying glass or a bunch of tweezers, presently is an incredible chance to utilize them. Some motherboards incorporate a connector that connects these jumpers to the correct associations on your motherboard. Something else, introducing them is as straightforward as coordinating the marks on the pins with the names on the associations.

The USB header interfacing with your forward looking motherboard ports will be all alone. This association is around eight by two pins, and they're encased in a bigger plastic lodging. This header has an indent on one side that ought to obviously show which course it connects.

STAGE SIX

Install the CPU cooler as well as warmth sinks

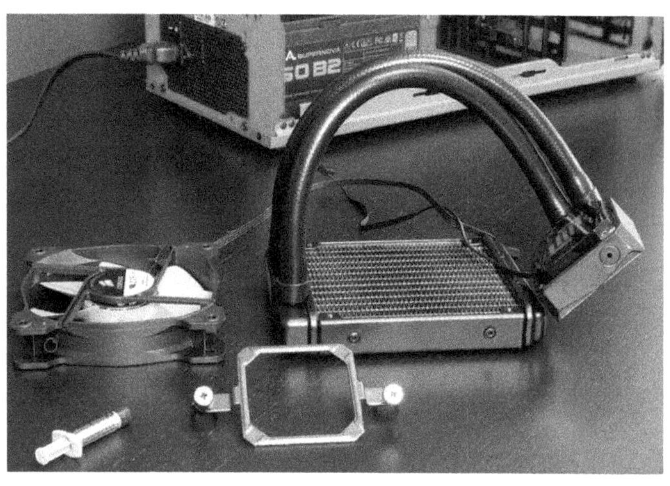

With the motherboard now fastened to your case, you can clear the perspiration of focus off your temple.

Establishment is less difficult when utilizing the CPU's bundled cooler. The cycle changes, be that as it may, given the various brands and ages. You'll have to allude to the included directions for explicit subtleties. The equivalent is valid for outsider coolers, which utilize a restrictive establishment section. Adhering to the included directions is vital to your PC-building achievement.

Each cooler requires warm glue. It's an incredible warm conductor, permitting warmth to move from the chip to the cooler easily. Without it, your cooler won't function admirably, if by any means. On the off chance that you don't know what kind of warm glue to utilize, it's well worth doing some exploration, and we have a rundown of the best warm glues for you to browse, as well.

AMD and Intel apply it to their coolers in the manufacturing plant, yet outsider coolers require manual gluing. Tragically, scouring goo on a costly CPU isn't as clear as it sounds

At the point when coordinated by the directions, essentially apply a solitary silver spot — about the size of a little pea — directly in the focal point of the chip. Subsequent to crushing the chip and cooler together, do whatever it takes not to squirm or bend excessively, to guarantee a smooth, full association. In case you're utilizing your own warm glue rather than what's pre-applied, try to completely clean the cooler utilizing espresso channels with a smidgen of isopropyl liquor, eliminating any hint of the recently applied glue.

For fundamental warmth sinks, you're currently completed; simply trust that the glue will fix. Be that as it may, the full fan framework actually needs power. Fitting the wires from the fan into a four-nail association with the motherboard, which ought to be near the processor and named "CPU FAN"

ASUS

STAGE SEVEN

Install your designs card

Only one out of every odd framework needs a devoted illustrations card (discrete GPU). On the off chance that you need an independent chip for illustrations, similar to PC gaming, establishment couldn't be less complex. We're likewise accepting for this progression that the card you picked is suitable for your case size, abilities, and force supply.

Present day illustrations cards utilize a PCI-Express (PCIe) x16 opening. It's a long, dainty connector situated on the back of the motherboard, beneath the processor. For by far most of motherboards, you'll need to utilize the top PCIe x16 space.

To situate the card in that opening, you'll need to eliminate a rectangular backplate from your nook. It's one of many meager metal sections lined down the rear of the case to keep it fixed up.

You'll have to eliminate a couple, contingent upon the card's width. Do this by eliminating the screw that tie down the backplate to the undercarriage. When eliminated, the plate should slide (or drop) out uninhibitedly. Keep the screw as you'll require it in a second.

Subsequent to eliminating the sections, do sure the switch on the motherboard's PCIe space is pushed outward. At that point, with the ports confronting the vacant spot where the backplate used to be, cautiously line up the long arrangement of contacts on the card with the suitable opening on the motherboard. Whenever it's arranged appropriately, a strong push on the highest point of the card should make it fit properly as the switch clicks back in to hold it.

You don't require inordinate power, yet on the off chance that you experience a lot of obstruction, look again at the backplate and PCIe space to make sure both are understood and the motherboard is appropriately adjusted. Likewise observe if there is a push-pin that secures the card like your memory spaces, as some motherboards use it as a wellbeing measure.

Utilize the screws pulled from the metal sections to attach the rear of the card into a similar spot for the situation. Once more, they don't should be amazingly close — barely to hold the card solidly set up.

The connector is intended to forestall inappropriate establishment, so if the association isn't simple, twofold check your arrangement to ensure its right.

Most video cards need additional force separated from what the PCIe space gives. In the event that your card needs additional juice, you'll see a PCIe power connector on the card's side confronting endlessly from the motherboard or, at times, as an afterthought confronting the front of the case. This connector is a gathering of square plastic pins numbering six or eight.

The most impressive cards may have two such connectors. Locate the suitable connector on your force supply, commonly named VGA, and space it in. The connector's plan forestalls ill-advised establishment, so if the association isn't simple, twofold check your arrangement to ensure its right. In the event that you need extra assistance, we have an itemized control on the most proficient method to introduce an illustrations card with extra data.

STAGE EIGHT

Install any extra development cards

Illustrations cards aren't the lone segments that utilization PCIe spaces. Other include cards incorporate remote systems administration, sound, video catch, and even capacity. Their establishment is the same than adding a discrete GPU.

To begin with, eliminate the metal section in the rear of the case that compares with the PCIe or other development space playing host to your include card. Keep the section screw convenient so you can utilize it to make sure about your new card.

PCIe openings have a little switch at the inside end, which you push down and outward to open the space. From that point onward, line up the column of contacts on the card with the opening and solidly push down. When you appropriately seat the card, the switch flips up. Making sure about the card set up is as basic as screwing it into the rear of the case and joining any important PCIe ports.

There are a couple of various sorts of PCIe openings. Numerous development cards utilize the "PCIe 4x" space, which is a lot more limited than the full PCIe opening utilized by video cards. A snappy check of your motherboard's availability, and the size of the connector on your card, will make it clear which space is proper. If all else fails, allude to the development card's manual.

STAGE NINE

Install your capacity drives

There are three diverse stockpiling drive sizes you're probably going to experience, and they all mount and interface in an unexpected way. For the most part, hard plate drives (HDD)

are the bigger 3.5-inch size, while more up to date strong state drives (SSD) receive the more modest 2.5-inch size. There's additionally the significantly more modest M.2 organization and PCI-Express drive design, which will in general be slight sticks with uncovered chips estimating around 1 x 3 inches.

We'll begin with 3.5-inch information drives, which are typically mounted up high at the front of the framework. Your case is nearly ensured to have at any rate one space devoted to this drive type. Establishment relies upon the fenced in area, notwithstanding, as most cases have a basic hard drive confine. Introducing a drive implies opening it into a mount on the pen and adjusting the screw openings on the drive's sides with those on the pen. Ensure the drive's force and information connectors face inwards, at the motherboard. When adjusted, screw the crash into place.

Present day cases usually appreciate a "instrument less" establishment framework. As the term infers, this plan should mean it's conceivable to introduce the drive without a screwdriver. Generally, this implies putting the crash into a support or pens that space into the case. Allude to your nook's guidelines for points of interest, since the method differs starting with one brand then onto the next.

For 2.5-inch drives, the mounting cycle and area change. A few cases have a pen, like the 3.5-inch mounting, where the SSD can simply slide in — no bolts, screws or sections required. On the off chance that it doesn't, the SSD requires a connector so it can sit safely in a 3.5-inch cove.

You can mount this drive in one of two different ways. Either the bigger section gives openings inside so you can screw the crash into the center, or the case incorporates a section that adds additional bigness to the 2.5-inch drive.

Hard drives require two associations also: One for force and one for information. Fortunately both are L-molded, so it's difficult to connect them some unacceptable opening or a misguided course.

For those with a more current M.2 drive, you'll need to search for a little opening that coordinates the width of your stick-formed drive, and a screw found a couple of inches away. Eliminate the screw, embed the contact end into the opening, and afterward push down delicately until you can utilize the screw to hold the drive set up once.

At long last, you can mount PCI-Express stockpiling drives much the same as you do with designs cards in an accessible PCI-Express space.

STAGE TEN

Make the last associations

Before you get too energized and hit that force button, it merits running back through the framework to ensure everything is appropriately situated and associated. We should begin with the parts.

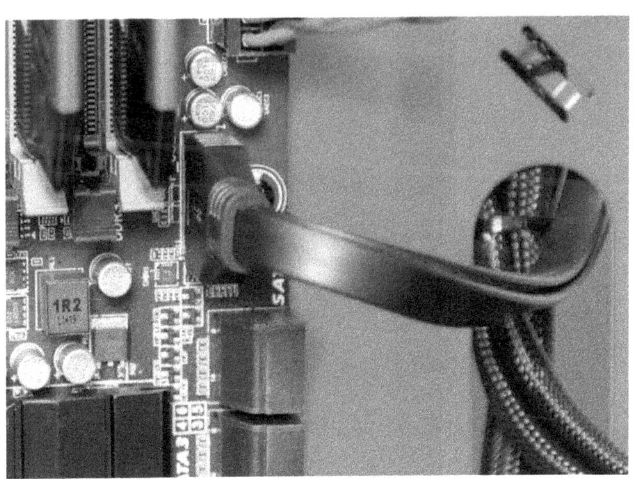

The motherboard is generally simple to spot in the event that it isn't connected. Most PSUs have one wide link that is clearly planned for this opening, with no different associations joined. It should plug into your board some place close to the PCIe spaces, however the area will shift.

Your motherboard is additionally prone to have a second, four-pin (or eight-pin) connector that controls the processor. You may have to glance through your force supply's accessible connectors with a sharp eye to think that it gives it looks like a PCIe power connector. In any case, don't stress — a PCIe connector won't fit, so inappropriate establishment is unimaginable.

The CPU cooler likewise needs power, yet that streams from the motherboard. Its force link doesn't have to go far, as most motherboards keep the fitting near the attachment. The little wire is only three or four attachments and interfaces with a bunch of four pins on the motherboard.

The hard drives need power too as L-molded SATA connectors (except if it's a PCIe drive). Ordinarily, a line of three or four lines run directly from the force supply utilizing novel connectors. You can't introduce them the incorrect way, by the same token.

At long last, powerful illustrations cards need committed force associations, ordinarily as a dark rectangular connector with six or eight pins. A few cards, similar to the new RTX 3080, even require two eight pin associations. These fittings are splendidly hued and simple to spot and just fit in the inside finish of the card in one direction. In the event that they aren't connected, the fans on the card won't turn, and it won't create any video yield.

STAGE ELEVEN

POWER ON

Since you've twofold checked everything, switch on the force supply and press the force button on the front. Great deals of frameworks don't boot accurately the first run through, so don't get debilitate in the event that you need to return and check associations once more.

When it boots, you'll need to introduce a working framework (OS). Fortunately, we've constructed a helpful guide that unmistakably aids you through the cycle. On the off chance that you don't have another PC around to download the ISO, you can buy a USB thumb drive from Microsoft with the OS picture all set.

From that point onward, you may have to introduce drivers. Windows 10 as of now underpins current chipsets and consequently downloads and introduces the excess drivers by and large. Check the Update and Security menu in the Settings sheet for more data with respect to this cycle.

In the event that that doesn't work, the chipset driver for your motherboard will deal with most network and locally available highlights, however this shifts extraordinarily dependent on motherboard and part producers. Make sure to check segment boxes for introduce plates and other data prior to tossing them out with the garbage.

Ordinarily, just discrete designs cards expect you to physically download and introduce the most recent driver. Look at the AMD page and get the Radeon drivers or the GeForce drivers.

With some karma and a great deal of tender loving care, you ought to have a completely operational framework. Make a point to look out for any mistake messages, and hold your hand outside the case fans to ensure wind streams and isn't excessively hot — at any rate for half a month.

On the off chance that something breaks or needs an overhaul, you're completely outfitted to manage it. Simply look out for static.

After you're finished structuring your PC, you'll be left with a wreck of boxes, unused links and connectors, and circles. Keep the containers or toss them out; the decision is yours. Nonetheless, we would suggest keeping your additional items coordinated. As you overhaul your PC, a fan-parting link or some additional warm glue will prove to be useful, and you'll discover these regularly packaged with CPU coolers and motherboards.

STAGE TWELVE

HOW TO INSTALL OPERATING SYSTEM ON A COMPUTER

This step below will show you how to install a computer operating system from scratch on a new computer. Windows Installation media is what you need to install it on a window computer. Mac computers that is purchase new brand will always come with an already installed operating system but can still be re-installed when a default.

INSTALLING OPERATING SYSTEM ON WINDOWS 10

A.

Create a media for Windows Installation

You can order for a Windows 10 on a newly built pc which an installation media might be sent to you.

If installation media does not exist on your window, make one for yourself

Get a computer that has access to internet, 8GB or 16GB USB flash drive. Know if the system architectural bit is 32 or 64 must be considered. The product key will only be gotten when you purchase Windows

Get window installation media by following these steps below;

Insert a USB drive with minimum capacity of 8 GB and good internet access computer. Back up any data on the USB drive to prevent losing it.

On the web browser, visit https://www.microsoft.com/en-us/software-download/windows10

You will click on the **Download Tool Now**.

Open and enter the portion showing "MediaCreationTool.exe" on a Downloads folder.

You will now Click **Accept**.

You will now click "Create Installation Media (DVD or ISO file) on another PC"

Then click on **Next**.

You will now on your language, the Windows edition, and the architecture of the PC

Then click "**Next**".

You will now click on "USB flash drive"

Click **Next**.

Next is clicking on USB drive

Click **Next**

B

Back up all your vital files

If Windows installation already exist on your computer, backup will become necessary so as to prevent losing your files. These files can be back up on these devices like One Drive and

Google Drive or any USB/hard disk storage device.

C

The Windows Installation Media can now be inserted on the computer you are about to install Windows on

Look for a free USB port and insert the menu for window installation on it

D

You will now boot the computer

You will restart the PC incase it has been powered on already by applying the normally restart method of the operating system on the PC.

If the PC is not powered on at the moment, apply a press on the power button to help boot it up.

E

Click on the Boot menu.

Booting menu resides in some new computer during booting up. The system motherboard determines how you start system booting. The listed keys below are the common way to reach the PC boot menu
F10, **F11**, **F12**, **F2**, or the use of
Esc when PC has already boots up. The

list of drives you want to boot will be listed here

Older PC enters the BIOS settings to boot up the PC. The button that pops up BIOS setting varies from one system to another. Once your system boot up, **F1 F2**, **F3**, **Esc** or the **Delete** keys are pressed to get the BIOS options from the menu of the window setting

F

Locate the USB drive

This drive is where the Windows Installation Media resides. In this case, the PC boots from the Windows Installation Media directly. Once the booting process of the computer begins from the USB drive, tap on any key to get the Windows installation on.

From the BIOS settings, search for **"Boot order"**, or "Priorities". You can now make a decision by changing the boot order so as to boot the PC from USB drive firstly. Click the save and exit option to quickly reboot the PC from USB drive.

G

Select your prefer language, time, currency, keyboard input and then click "Next".

You can easily select your language, country, and the keyboard input method with the aid of drop down menu.

You can now tap “**Next**”.

H

Tap on Install Now

Tap the center button on the screen to install it.

I

You will now enter the Windows product key

Tap on **Next**

If window has already been purchased, expect the license key to appear as confirmation on your email. If you are yet to purchase a Windows, tap the display showing **“I don't have a product key”**. You will purchase Windows and try to activate it.

J

Select the Windows you desire to install and click the option displaying “Next”.

If you have window already purchased, try to click the correct version of window.

If you are yet to purchase Windows, select the version that will suit your installation. Different window versions come with different prices.

If you do not know the window version to install, Windows Home Edition is taken as the most accepted window version.

K

The checkbox closer to "I accept the license terms" should be click.

Click on **"Next"** You will read all the license terms displayed at center of the window. If you are set to continue, tap the option that displays next.

L

Click on “Custom”: and the Install Windows only or Upgrade

You will now Install Windows with the file settings, and applications.

If window is install on your PC already, click on upgrade to install window and other files settings.

If window does not exist on the PC before, click “custom” and install window as the only option.

M

Choose the drive/partition you decide to install the Windows on.

Click on **"Delete"** If you have several hard drives, choose the one you want to partition for window installation.

Tap the option that displays **"Delete".**

Note that this action erases all data available on the drive. Back up your vital information on the drive to avoid losing information.

N
Choose the drive with an unallocated space.

Tap on **"Next"** to see the installing Windows begins on the drive you just selected. This process will take a required amount of time depending on the hardware space of your computer.

o

The USB flash drive can now be removed to restart your computer

System automatically restarts when window installation is complete. The USB flash drive is removed so that booting do not take place again from the Flash drive. Booting window at the first time does not pass through the Setup stages.

STAGE THIRTEEN

CONCLUSION

It is good for you to know how to build your own computer for gaming or any other information communication purposes. The maintenance process of your computer will be easily since you built it from the scratch.

You tell your friends with boldness that you built a working computer and it makes them to see you as a professional.

For you to be better in building a computer for gaming or for other functions, you need to engage more in computer building and software installation

THE END

www.ingramcontent.com/pod-product-compliance
Ingram Content Group UK Ltd.
Pitfield, Milton Keynes, MK11 3LW, UK
UKHW021934190726
13853UKWH00004B/1448